EXPLORING WORLD CULTURES

Portugal

Alicia Z. Klepeis

Cavendish
Square
New York

Published in 2018 by Cavendish Square Publishing, LLC
243 5th Avenue, Suite 136, New York, NY 10016

First Edition

Website: cavendishsq.com

This publication represents the opinions and views of the author based on his or her personal experience, knowledge, and research. The information in this book serves as a general guide only. The author and publisher have used their best efforts in preparing this book and disclaim liability rising directly or indirectly from the use and application of this book.

All websites were available and accurate when this book was sent to press.

Library of Congress Cataloging-in-Publication Data

Names: Klepeis, Alicia, 1971- author.
Title: Portugal / Alicia Z. Klepeis.
Description: New York : Cavendish Square Publishing, 2018. |
Series: Exploring world cultures | Includes index.
Identifiers: LCCN 2017013866 (print) | LCCN 2017015097 (ebook) |
ISBN 9781502630261 (E-book) | ISBN 9781502630254 (library bound) |
ISBN 9781502630230 (pbk.) | ISBN 9781502630247 (6 pack)
Subjects: LCSH: Portugal--Juvenile literature.
Classification: LCC DP517 (ebook) | LCC DP517 .K54 2018 (print) |
DDC 946.9--dc23
LC record available at https://lccn.loc.gov/2017013866

Editorial Director: David McNamara
Editor: Kristen Susienka
Copy Editor: Alex Tessman
Associate Art Director: Amy Greenan
Designer: Graham Abbott
Production Coordinator: Karol Szymczuk
Photo Research: J8 Media

Printed in the United States of America

Contents

Introduction

Portugal is a country in Europe. It has many special celebrations and traditions.

People have lived in Portugal for thousands of years. Different groups have ruled what is now Portugal during its history. Two examples are the Romans and the Moors. Today Portugal is a free country. Its government is a **democracy**.

People in Portugal have many kinds of jobs. Some work in hotels, hospitals, or schools. Others make cars or catch fish from the sea. Portuguese farmers grow many types of food on their land.

Portugal has lots of beautiful places to visit. It has beaches, mountains, forests, and ponds.

Visitors come from around the world to see Portugal's historical sites and lovely scenery.

Portuguese people value the arts, literature, and music. They also enjoy playing sports and eating good food. They have many festivals and celebrations during the year.

Portugal is an amazing country to explore.

Traditional boats sit on Portugal's Duoro River in Porto.

Geography

Portugal is part of Europe. It is a little smaller than the state of Indiana. The country covers 35,556 square miles (92,090 square kilometers).

A map of Portugal

Portugal is located on the Iberian Peninsula in western Europe. Portugal only borders one other country, Spain. The Atlantic Ocean is to the west. The Gulf of Cádiz lies to its south.

Mountains and **plateaus** form much of northern Portugal. The Estrela Mountain range is located here. There are many plains and rolling hills in southern Portugal.

Portugal's Animals and Plants

Portugal is home to many different plants and animals. Cork trees and wild orchids grow here. Chameleons, deer, and flamingoes live here too.

A greenfinch

The Rio Tejo begins in Spain and runs through Portugal. It empties into the Atlantic Ocean. This river divides the country into two halves.

Portugal controls two **archipelagos**. The Azores lie west of Portugal in the Atlantic Ocean. The Madeira islands are off the northwest coast of Africa.

FACT!

Portugal has a **maritime** climate. It is rainy and cool in the north but warmer and drier in the south.

7

History

The Moorish Fountain was designed in 1922.

People have lived in what is now Portugal for thousands of years. Throughout its history, there have been many groups of people here. The Celts, Phoenicians, and Romans were some early settlers.

During the 700s CE, a group called the Moors came to Portugal from North Africa. Many of these newcomers were Muslim. They brought new foods, art forms, and styles of architecture to Portugal.

The Christians living in Portugal fought with the Moors. In 1139, Portugal became independent.

FACT!

In 1755, a huge earthquake destroyed Portugal's capital, Lisbon. It took many years to rebuild the city.

King Alfonso I ruled the country then. In the 1400s, Portuguese explorers set out on voyages around the globe. Over time, Portugal became a world power. It had colonies in Africa, South America, and Asia.

Portugal's government changed hands many times during the twentieth century. The country became a **republic** in 1910. From 1932 to 1968, a dictator named Antonio de Oliveira Salazar ruled Portugal. The country became a democracy in 1974. It has been free ever since.

The Navigator

Prince Henry

Prince Henry the Navigator was a Portuguese leader during the 1400s. He wanted to find new sea travel routes and encouraged exploration of the world.

VOTE ✓

Portugal is a democracy. It has eighteen districts and two **autonomous** regions. The capital of Portugal is Lisbon.

The São Bento Palace in Lisbon.

Portugal's government has three parts:

1) Legislative: In Portugal, this part of the government is called the Assembly of the Republic. People in this group write new laws.

2) Judicial: The courts make up this part of Portugal's government. They follow the country's

FACT!

All Portuguese citizens over the age of eighteen can vote in elections.

constitution. The constitution was signed in 1976. It describes all the basic laws of Portugal.

3) Executive: The president, prime minister, and Council of Ministers make up this part of the government.

Portugal's Assembly of the Republic is made up of one area, or house. It has 230 members. They gather in the São Bento Palace in Lisbon to pass laws.

Women in Government

About 35 percent of the members of Portugal's Assembly of the Republic are women.

The Economy

Portugal does not have the biggest economy in Europe, but it trades with countries around the world. Its most important trading partners include Spain, France, and Germany. Its money is called the euro.

Portuguese euros

About two-thirds of Portuguese workers have service jobs. Some work in hotels, banks, and hospitals. Others have jobs in shops, schools, and museums.

Portuguese workers make many different products. Some are basic, like footwear or clothing. But others are high-tech. These include

Over ten million tourists visited Portugal in 2015.

Portuguese fishermen sort through the day's catch.

cars, electronics, and communications equipment.

With its long coastlines, Portuguese fishermen gather food from the sea. In the countryside, farmers grow lots of crops. Grains, potatoes, and tomatoes are a few. The country also produces olive oil and wine. Workers called miners dig minerals from under Earth's surface. Tin, copper, and zinc are some examples.

Put a Cork In It!

Portugal is the world's largest producer of cork. Cork is often used as a stopper in wine bottles.

Portugal's people, animals, and plants need clean water and air to live. Some places in Portugal do not have these things.

A wild fox sleeps in northern Portugal.

In 2016, air pollution here was worse than in recent years. Why? Forest fires and dust blown from the Sahara Desert caused some of this pollution.

Some Portuguese cities like Lisbon also suffer from air pollution. Car traffic creates lots of this type of pollution.

The government is working to ban older cars from driving in the city's downtown during certain times of the day. This is because older cars can pollute more than newer ones.

The Mediterranean monk seal and the Iberian wolf are two endangered animals living in Portugal.

The water in Portugal is mostly clean. Some places, like the coast, do have water pollution.

Some of this pollution comes from chemicals used in farming or industrial emissions.

Portugal and Energy

Portugal is a world leader in clean energy. It gets about 28 percent of its electricity from water power. Another 29 percent comes from other clean sources like the wind or the sun.

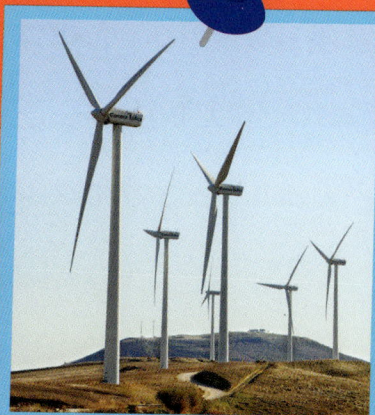
These windmills are making power.

Over ten million people live in Portugal. The country's population is one of the most **homogeneous** in Europe. Most people are of a Mediterranean background. They share a common culture.

Two girls take part in the April Flower Festival in Madeira.

There are other people in Portugal too. For centuries, Portugal had colonies around the world. Less than one hundred thousand people of black African ancestry came to Portugal as its colonies gained independence. Brazilians, Chinese, and other people also moved here.

Over the last couple of decades, people have moved to Portugal from many countries. Many people from Ukraine, Cape Verde, and Romania now call Portugal home. Small numbers of refugees have moved in from war-torn areas of the world. All of these newcomers have brought their own traditions, foods, and languages to Portugal.

The Roma

The Roma are a group of people in Portugal. Originally the Roma came to Europe from India. They often move from place to place and live differently from most Portuguese people.

People in Portugal live in different ways. More than 60 percent of Portugal's people live in cities and towns. Some live in houses. Others live in apartments. Portuguese folks in the city might ride the bus or a tram to work.

A tram in Lisbon's city center

Families in cities often have computers and cell phones. Some also own cars. Some Portuguese people work as miners in rural areas. Others have jobs at nature parks. People in Portugal's countryside often lead slower-paced lives. Some grow crops for food or to sell. A farmer might live in a tile-roofed house and have an olive grove in his or her yard. Other farmers raise animals or host tourists at their farms.

Many Portuguese women today work outside of the home. They have jobs as businesspeople, doctors, bankers, teachers, shopkeepers, and more.

Produce

While Portugal does have big supermarkets, people often shop at local markets. Here people can buy everything from fruits and vegetables to meat and flowers.

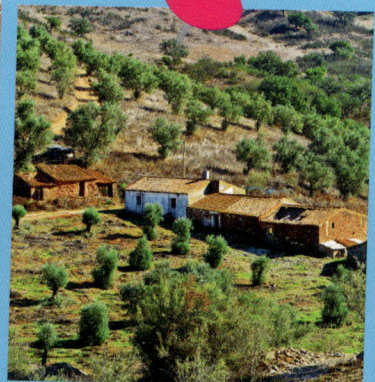

Olives grow on a Portuguese farm.

Religion

Religion is very important to many Portuguese people. Portugal has no official religion. All people are free to believe in what they want. However, many people here are Christian. About 81 percent of Portugal's population are Roman Catholic.

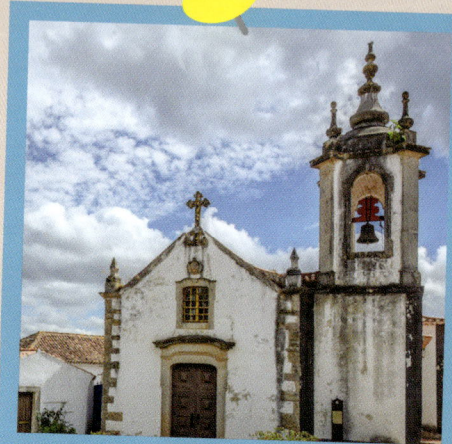

A church stands in Obidos, Portugal.

Christian church services are held every Sunday in villages and cities across Portugal. Some people attend every week, but many do not. Like other Christians, those in Portugal celebrate certain holidays like Easter and Christmas. Throughout the countryside, religious festivals take place all year long. Many celebrate saints.

Less than 1 percent of Portugal's people follow a religion other than Christianity. Some are Jewish or Muslim, for example.

FACT!

Almost 7 percent of Portugal's people do not follow any religion at all.

All Saints' Day

All Saints' Day is an important religious holiday in Portugal. On that day, people remember family members who have died. Many visit the cemeteries where their relatives are buried.

On All Saints' Day, a couple visits a grave.

Language

Portuguese is the most commonly spoken language in Portugal. It is also an official language of Portugal. The country's government uses Portuguese. People often speak Portuguese for business matters and in schools. Many professionals and businesspeople also speak English. In fact, about 32 percent of the people in Portugal speak English.

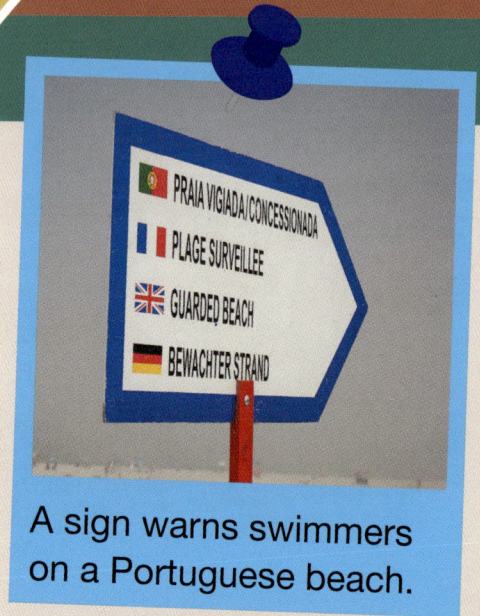

A sign warns swimmers on a Portuguese beach.

FACT!

More than 190 million people around the world speak Portuguese.

Portugal has a second official language called Mirandese. This language only became an official language in 1999. Mirandese is not commonly spoken in Portugal. In fact, only about ten to fifteen thousand people speak it. Most of them live in the northeast corner of the country.

People in Portugal often learn to speak more than one language. Schools here commonly teach children English and French. Also, immigrants who have come to Portugal from different places may speak languages other than Portuguese.

Learn a Little Portuguese

If you want to say "hello," say *ola* (OH-lah). To say "thank you," say *obrigado* (oh-bree-GAH-doh).

All over Portugal people enjoy the arts. Some artists create paintings or sculptures. Josefa de Óbidos is a famous painter from the seventeenth century. Her works have been

Fado musicians perform.

shown in museums around the world.

Music is another important part of Portuguese culture. **Fado** is a kind of folk music here. People make fado music using stringed instruments known as the *guitarra* and viola, and by singing.

Portugal has festivals throughout the year. Portuguese people celebrate Portugal Day on

October 5 is Republic Day. This Portuguese holiday celebrates the end of the monarchy and the beginning of the country as a republic. On this day there are parades and people wave flags.

June 10. This national holiday is also called Camões Day in honor of the Portuguese poet Luís Vaz de Camões. He wrote poems about the nation's journeys of exploration.

Tile Style

Lisbon is home to a National Tile Museum. Portugal is famous for its beautiful blue and white tiles called *azulejos*. These tiles decorate buildings across the country.

Fun and Play

There are many ways to have fun in Portugal. Lots of Portuguese people enjoy sports. The most popular sport is soccer (called *futebol*). Basketball is also well liked here. Just like in the United States, Portugal has professional soccer and basketball leagues.

Ships sail in the blue waters of Portugal's Algarve region.

With its long coastline, water sports are popular in Portugal. People here enjoy swimming. Local people and tourists visiting Portugal also sail and scuba dive.

Many people in Portugal like to play games. Outdoor activities include hopscotch, jumping

Cristiano Ronaldo is probably the biggest soccer star from Portugal. He has played for Real Madrid and Manchester United.

rope, and sack races. There's also a game called *jogo do pião*. In this game, players throw a spinning top to the floor. They try to knock over the other players' tops.

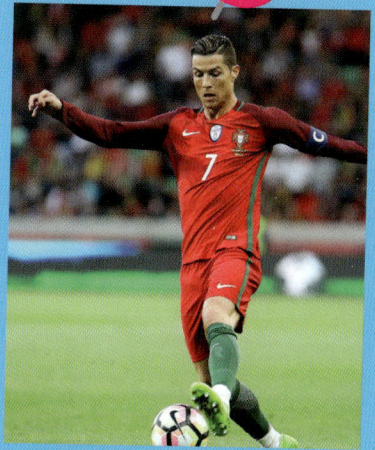
Cristiano Ronaldo

Bullfighting

Bullfighting is a traditional sport in Portugal. Some people enjoy watching the bullfighter battle the bull. Others feel this sport is cruel to the animals.

Food

People in Portugal eat lots of different kinds of food. Portuguese cooks use many spices in their dishes. Cinnamon, pepper, and curry powder are all popular spices here.

Bacalhau, the national dish of Portugal

Seafood is often on the menu in Portugal. People here eat all types of seafood—from octopus to cuttlefish to tuna. The country's national dish

FACT!

Goat stew is a specialty more popular in Portugal's inland areas. Rabbit is another meat more commonly prepared in the Portuguese countryside.

is called *bacalhau*, or salted codfish. There are many different ways to prepare this dish.

People in Portugal also enjoy pork dishes, meaty stews, and soups. It's common to serve meals with potatoes, rice, and salad. Sometimes people eat cheeses before or after a main meal.

Portuguese people have access to many types of fruits such as grapes, apricots, and pears. Tea, coffee, and wine are popular beverages here.

Desserts in Portugal

Portugal offers many desserts to people who enjoy sweets. Rice pudding sprinkled with cinnamon is a favorite. Custard tarts are well liked too.

Glossary

archipelago	A group or chain of islands.
autonomous	A region that governs itself.
democracy	A system of government in which leaders are chosen by the people.
fado	A type of Portuguese folk music involving stringed instruments and singing.
homogeneous	Being of a similar kind or sharing a culture and heritage.
maritime	Referring to a climate that is temperate and moist because of the influence of the sea.
plateau	A broad flat area of high ground.
republic	A government where people have the right to vote.

Find Out More

Books

Deckker, Zilah. *Portugal*. Countries of the World. Washington, DC: National Geographic Children's Books, 2009.

Schuetz, Kari. *Portugal*. Exploring Countries. Minneapolis, MN: Bellwether Media, 2012.

Website

TIME: A Day in the Life: Portugal

http://www.timeforkids.com/destination/portugal/day-in-life

Video

Excitement in the Azores

http://www.travelchannel.com/destinations/portugal/video/excitement-in-the-azores

This video shares the Azores islands and all of their natural beauty.

Index

About the Author

Alicia Z. Klepeis began her career at the National Geographic Society. She is the author of many kids' books, including *Haunted Cemeteries Around the World*, *Bizarre Things We've Called Medicine*, and *A Time For Change*. She lives with her family in upstate New York.